SEP -- 202

STARK LIBRARY

WOMEN WHO MADE HISTORY

WRITERS AND ARTISTS

Written by
JULIA ADAMS

Illustrated by
LOUISE WRIGHT

Gareth Stevens
PUBLISHING

Anne Frank
(page 14)

Please visit our website, www.garethstevens.com. For a free color catalog of all our high-quality books, call toll free 1-800-542-2595 or fax 1-877-542-2596.

Cataloging-in-Publication Data

Names: Adams, Julia. | Wright, Louise.
Title: Writers and artists / Julia Adams, illustrated by Louise Wright.
Description: New York : Gareth Stevens Publishing, 2020.
| Series: Women who made history | Includes glossary and index.
Identifiers: ISBN 9781538243091 (pbk.) | ISBN 9781538243107 (library bound)
Subjects: LCSH: Women authors–Biography–Juvenile literature.
| Women artists–Biography–Juvenile literature.
Classification: LCC PN471.A33 2020 | DDC 809'.89287 B–dc23

First Edition

Published in 2020 by
Gareth Stevens Publishing
111 East 14th Street, Suite 349
New York, NY 10003

Copyright © Arcturus Holdings Ltd, 2020

Author: Julia Adams
Illustrator: Louise Wright
Designer: Sally Bond
Editor: Susannah Bailey

All rights reserved. No part of this book may be reproduced in any form without permission in writing from the publisher, except by a reviewer.

Printed in the United States of America

CPSIA compliance information: Batch #CS19GS: For further information contact Gareth Stevens, New York, New York at 1-800-542-2595.

Bjork
(page 22)

CONTENTS

Awesome Women	4	Miriam Mekeba	20
Artists and Writers	6	Björk	22
Making History	8	Virginia Woolf	23
Nina Simone	10	Frida Kahlo	24
Sonita Alizadeh	12	Simone de Beauvoir	26
Joan Armatrading	13	Joanne (J.K.) Rowling	28
Anne Frank	14	Xian Zhang	29
Kiri Te Kanawa	16	Arundhati Roy	30
Angelina Jolie	17	Maya Angelou	32
Nadežda Petrović	18	Laverne Cox	34
Melba Liston	19	Maria Callas	35
		Millo Castro Zaldarriaga	36
		Grace Cossington Smith	37
		Coco Chanel	38
		Zaha Hadid	40
		Quiz	42
		Research Poject	43
		Glossary	44
		Further Information	46
		Index	48

Laverne Cox
(page 34)

AWESOME WOMEN

The course of history is packed with stories of women overcoming odds, defying expectations, and shattering stereotypes. Yet, all too often, their contribution has been overlooked, underplayed, or just forgotten.

Melba Liston (page 19)

Many cultures have believed (or still believe) that women do not need an education, cannot be trusted with leadership, are physically inferior, and are intellectually weak. Men have been privileged, and this means that they have been the world's default decision-makers and history writers. Women, however, have been achieving greatness even when everything seemed against them.

Grace Cossington Smith (page 37)

The writers and artists in this book are by no means the definitive list of female historymakers, nor are they perfect and without fault, but they are pioneers who stood out, made a difference, and proved without a doubt that they were just as capable as men. Their contributions, both to their field and as an inspiration to others, are worthy of celebration. And that is what this book aims to do.

Frida Kahlo
(page 24)

ARTISTS AND WRITERS

Angelina Jolie
(page 17)

Art is part of being human. It includes visual arts, such as painting, photography, and film; literary arts, including novels, poems, and plays; and performing arts, such as music, drama, and dance. In all its forms, art helps us to explore our identity and express feelings and big ideas.

Great artists can be men or women, but in many cultures success has been easier for men. Women authors have even chosen to write under male names to increase their chance of

Virginia Woolf
(page 23)

being published and read. George Eliot's real name, for example, was Mary Ann Evans.

Being poor can make it harder to be an artist. Having music lessons, going to the ballet, or being able to access lots of books all cost money. As a result, the arts can lack voices from their most disadvantaged members —but thankfully there are exceptions. The women in this book are writers, poets, singers, musicians, designers, painters, and actors. Many of them came to their art because they needed to express themselves and their position in society. Being an artist and an activist often go hand in hand. Women have harnessed the power of art to comment on society, challenge wrong or harmful ideas, and nudge or catapult us toward change.

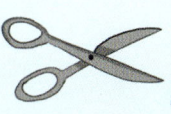

Zaha Hadid (page 40)

7

MAKING HISTORY

In the past, it was usual for men to be educated to a high degree, and women were only educated enough to make interesting conversation in company. Women were often taught music and painting, but only as an entertainment, not an art form. Many women, however, stand out in the past for going above and beyond their education and what was usual at the time they lived.

JANE AUSTEN
(1775 – 1817)

Since the 19th century, Jane Austen has been one of Britain's most popular novelists. Her works, which include *Pride and Prejudice* and *Emma*, have been turned into films and television series many times. Jane's witty words described life for women in the middle and upper classes and drew out truths that are still relevant to this day.

Jane grew up in a close, happy family, with seven brothers and sisters. Her own experiences and the lives of her family informed her writing. Jane wrote stories, sketches, and poems from a young age, and when she had written her first novel, *Sense and Sensibility*, her brother helped her to get it published. Four novels were published in her lifetime, and two after her death. They were all published anonymously, simply "By a Lady."

"One of the things about this extraordinary instrument that I have is the blackness in it, the natural flavor. It's something extra."

LEONTYNE PRICE
(b.1927)

Soprano singer Leontyne Price was the first African American to be a leading artist at the Metropolitan Opera in New York City. She had to overcome many obstacles. Leontyne's 1961 debut at the Met was greeted with more than 40 minutes of nonstop applause.

Leontyne grew up in a small town in Mississippi at a time when society was still segregated by race. Her mother sang in church and took her to a concert by a great contralto singer. From that moment, Leontyne knew she wanted to be a singer.

Leontyne first appeared on stage in 1957, and was then central to the opening in 1966 of the new Met theater. She continued to sing opera until 1985 when she retired, but continued to give concerts. She even appeared in a film about the Metropolitan Opera House at the age of 90.

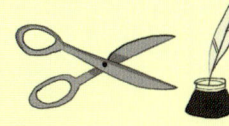

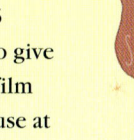

NINA SIMONE
Musician, Singer, and Activist
(1933–2003)

Nina Simone (born Eunice Kathleen Waymon) was from North Carolina. Her mother was a Baptist minister and her father was a maintenance worker and preacher. Nina was only three years old when she started playing songs on the organ in her mother's church.

Recognizing her incredible talent, Nina's parents sent her to piano lessons. She was a natural and decided to become the first black classical pianist. Her hometown raised money to fund her time at high school and then Juilliard, New York City's leading school for music and dance.

Nina grew up at a time of terrible racial discrimination. Slavery had been abolished in 1865, but many states, especially southern ones,

"You can't help it. An artist's duty, as far as I'm concerned, is to reflect the times."

had segregation. Black citizens weren't allowed to share public spaces with white people. The civil rights movement in the 1960s worked to change this through peaceful protests and campaigning.

Being exposed to unfairness and racism throughout her life shaped Nina as an artist. When she was 12 years old, she gave her first piano recital. Her parents, who were seated in the front row, were asked to move to make space for white audience members. Nina refused to play until her parents were given back their seats.

Nina gave up her hopes of becoming a classical pianist in 1951, when she was rejected by the prestigious Curtis Institute of Music in Philadelphia. It was a disappointment, but it led to Nina's amazing career as one her century's most celebrated musicians and singers.

In 1954, Nina started working as a musician in a bar. She adopted the stage name "Nina Simone" to keep her mother from finding out—she wouldn't have approved! Nina's rich voice and her soulful versions of much-loved songs made her a popular fixture.

Nina released her first album in 1958. It was a big success but she had sold the creative rights to the record company. None of the profits went to her. In the 1960s, Nina joined the fight for civil rights and sang songs at rallies.

Frustrated by the racism in the United States, Nina spent most of the 1970s in Barbados, Africa, and Europe. In 1987, she reached a new generation when her recording of "My Baby Just Cares for Me" accompanied a high-profile perfume advertisement. In 1991, Nina published her autobiography, *I Put a Spell on You*. She spent the last 10 years of her life in southern France. Thanks to her extraordinary voice and accomplished piano playing, Nina has inspired many young musicians.

SONITA ALIZADEH

Rap Artist and Activist

(b.1997)

In 2014, the filmmaker Rokhsareh Ghaemmaghami started documenting the lives of refugees in her native Iran. She met a teenager called Sonita Alizadeh, who had fled her home country of Afghanistan when war broke out there. Rokhsareh began filming Sonita. As a result, she caught on camera the moment when Sonita's mother said she had found a husband to buy her.

"To the women of my beloved country: believe in yourselves. You are strong. Speak up about your dreams and your goals every day so that everyone knows that you exist"

Although the sale of brides is common in Afghanistan, Sonita was shocked that it was going to happen to her. She was just 16 years old. She expressed her fear and despair in a rap song called "Brides for Sale." Rokhsareh filmed the video for the song. When it was uploaded to YouTube, "Brides for Sale" went viral.

Rokhsareh paid Sonita's family to delay the marriage and helped her travel to Utah, where a high school was offering her a scholarship. The Strongheart Group, which is dedicated to social change, also gave Sonita financial support. She continues to raise awareness of child marriage.

Rokhsareh's film *Sonita* was released in 2016 and won an award at the Sundance Film Festival in Park City, Utah.

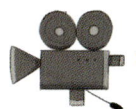

JOAN ARMATRADING
MUSICIAN, SINGER, AND SONGWRITER
(b.1950)

When Joan Armatrading was 14, she saw a secondhand guitar in a shop window and begged her mother to buy it. Her mother swapped two baby strollers for it, and Joan became the proud owner of her first guitar. She taught herself to play and started writing songs. Within two years she was playing her first gig.

Born on the Caribbean island of St. Kitts, Joan moved to Birmingham, UK, with her family when she was seven years old. Her musical talent was evident early on, when she started playing her mother's piano as a young child. Once she discovered the guitar, she embarked on a lifelong career as a singer, songwriter, and musician.

In 1972, Joan released her debut album and became the first black British female artist to find success with her own material. Since then she has released more than 20 solo albums. Her records have gone gold (sold 500,000 copies) and platinum (sold a million). She has been nominated for three Grammy Awards and two Brits.

In 2001, Joan was made a Member of the Order of the British Empire (MBE). She gained a history degree the same year. Joan supports many charities, especially ones that help young people.

PLATINUM RECORD

"You don't have to be rich and famous. You just have to be an ordinary person, doing extraordinary things."

ANNE FRANK
WRITER
(1929–45)

Born into a Jewish family, Anne Frank spent the first years of her childhood with her parents and older sister Margot in the German city of Frankfurt. When dictator Adolf Hitler came to power in 1933, Jewish people were suddenly discriminated against. The Frank family moved to Amsterdam in the Netherlands to avoid persecution.

The family soon settled. Anne's father Otto started his own business, the girls went to a local school, and Anne's mother Edith took care of the house. As war loomed, the Franks tried to emigrate but they were too late. Germany invaded Poland and World War II began.

In 1940, German troops marched into the Netherlands. Once more the Frank family faced anti-Semitic (anti-Jewish) laws. Margot and Anne had to attend schools for Jewish children and their father had to give up his business. Otto tried again to move his family to the United States, but it was just not possible.

In 1942, Otto built a hideout behind a bookcase at the back of his shop. The family planned to go into hiding in mid July, but they moved the date up after receiving a letter for Margot from the German government. It told her she must return at once to Germany and report to a work camp. Later that year, four more Jewish people joined them in their secret hiding place.

Only six trusted friends knew where the family was. They had all worked for Anne's father. They kept the Franks safe; brought them food, clothing, and books; and were their only contact with the outside world.

Anne kept a diary that documented her experiences. She wrote about everyday life in hiding, composed short stories, and collected quotes that she liked.

Life continued in this way until 1944 when someone informed the authorities. The Gestapo (Nazi secret police) raided the building, found the hideout, and arrested everyone. Anne and Margot were transported to Bergen-Belsen concentration camp; their parents were separated and sent to Auschwitz.

Otto was the only member of the family who survived the war. When he returned to Amsterdam his friend Miep Giess gave him Anne's diary, which she had found after the raid and kept safe. Otto was deeply moved by his daughter's writing and decided to publish it.

Since that time, Anne Frank's diary has been translated into more than 70 languages and has sold more than 30 million copies. It is one of the most powerful and moving pieces of wartime literature ever written.

"I still believe, in spite of everything, that people are really good at heart."

KIRI TE KANAWA
Opera Singer
(b.1944)

New Zealander Kiri Te Kanawa, who is part Maori, was taught to sing at high school. She shot to fame in 1971 with a part in The Marriage of Figaro at the Royal Opera House in London, UK. One of Kiri's proudest moments during a long and successful career was being heard by more than 600 million people worldwide when she sang at the wedding of Prince Charles and Lady Diana Spencer in 1981. She was made a Dame Commander of the Order of the British Empire (OBE) in 1982.

Kiri retired from singing in 2017 to focus on the Kiri Te Kanawa Foundation. She set up this organization in 2004 to support and teach talented young singers from New Zealand.

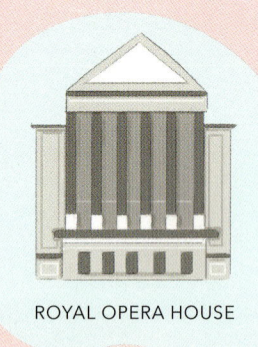

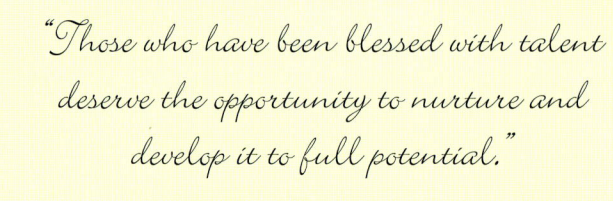

ROYAL OPERA HOUSE

"Those who have been blessed with talent deserve the opportunity to nurture and develop it to full potential."

ANGELINA JOLIE
ACTOR AND ACTIVIST
(b.1975)

Angelina Jolie Voight was born in Los Angeles. She made her screen debut at age seven in a movie starring her father, actor Jon Voight, but her breakthrough role was in *Hackers* (1995). Angelina won her first Golden Globe in 1998 and picked up an Oscar in 2000.

Angelina is a humanitarian activist as well as a successful actor. When she was a UN Goodwill Ambassador, she trained as a pilot so she could deliver aid to refugee camps. In 2012, Angelina was given diplomatic powers when she became a UN Special Envoy. She is also involved in community development, promoting human rights, and conserving habitats.

"We do not only want freedom and human rights for every single person in our own society, we want that for every other person in the world."

NADEŽDA PETROVIĆ
Painter
(1873–1915)

Born in Čačak, Serbia, Nadežda Petrović showed promise as a painter when she was still a teenager. She trained as an art teacher and then studied in Munich, Germany, where she met up-and-coming artists including Paul Klee and Wassily Kandinsky.

Her first solo exhibition took place in Belgrade in 1900. Over the next decade or so, Nadežda made a name for herself for her impressionist and wild style.

When the Balkan Wars (1912–1913) broke out, Nadežda volunteered as a nurse with the Red Cross and earned a Medal for Bravery. She had to stop in 1913 after catching typhus and cholera. Nadežda also served as a nurse with the Serbian army in World War I until she died of typhus in 1915.

Nadežda is featured on one of the Serbian banknotes. She is described as "one of the most important figures in Serbian art." There is also an art gallery named after her in Cacak, Serbia. They hold regular memorial exhibitions to remember her.

MELBA LISTON
MUSICIAN
(1926–1999)

"When I saw the trombone I thought how beautiful it looked and knew I just had to have one. No one told me that it was difficult to master. All I knew was that it was pretty and I wanted one."

Born in Kansas City, Missouri, Melba Liston came from a musical family. She started to teach herself the trombone when she was seven years old and joined her school band. Within a year she was performing a solo on the local radio. When Melba was 10 the family moved to Los Angeles, and she began to have private trombone lessons.

Melba began her career as a professional trombonist when she was 16. She toured with successful big band masters such as Dizzy Gillespie and earned respect in the male-dominated world of jazz. In later life, Melba became a composer, arranger, and producer for soul-music artists including Marvin Gaye and the Supremes.

MIRIAM MAKEBA
SINGER AND ACTIVIST
(1932–2008)

When Zenzile Miriam Makeba was born, no one could have believed that she would grow up to be one of the first African singers to find international fame. Her home was a poor township on the outskirts of Johannesburg, South Africa, and her parents were from different ethnic backgrounds—her father was Xhosa and her mother was Swazi.

When Miriam was only six years old, her father died suddenly. She had to take on cleaning and babysitting jobs to help to make money for the family. Miriam had already discovered her musical gift and was singing in the choir at school and church. She grew up believing that music would lift her out of poverty one day.

In 1948, the South African government introduced apartheid, a system to keep white and black people separate. Good homes and jobs were not available for black people like Miriam. They could not even share public spaces with white people.

Miriam became a professional singer in the 1950s. She toured southern Africa with a group called the Manhattan Brothers and also formed her own all-female group called the Skylarks.

In 1958, Miriam had a role in an anti-apartheid film called *Come Back, Africa*. It wasn't a big part, but she sang in it, and audiences loved her voice.

Miriam flew to New York City, and found jobs singing in jazz bars. A calypso singer called Harry Belafonte became her mentor and encouraged her to make her first recordings.

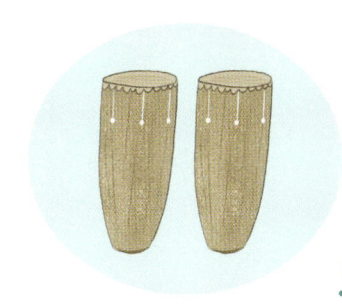

> "Girls are the future mothers of our society, and it is important that we focus on their well-being."

In 1960, the South African police shot at black protestors in a township called Sharpeville. They killed 69 people and injured 220. Miriam's mother died in the massacre. Miriam tried to return to home for her mother's funeral, but she discovered that she had been banned. It was the start of 31 years in exile.

It was an extraordinary time to be black and living in New York City. The African American civil rights movement was at its peak. Miriam became involved, but above all she spoke out against apartheid in her home country. At the same time, her musical career was taking off.

In 1990, Miriam returned to South Africa. Apartheid was now outlawed and the anti-apartheid activist Nelson Mandela had been released after 27 years in prison.

Known as "Mama Africa," Miriam became a Goodwill Ambassador for the UN in 1999 and was awarded the Otto Hahn Peace Medal in Gold in 2001. She died in Italy during her farewell musical tour.

BJÖRK
Musician, Singer, and Actor
(b.1965)

Known only by her first name, Björk Guðmundsdóttir was born in Reykjavik, Iceland. Her musical career started early—she recorded her first solo album at 11 years old and spent her teens in various bands. From 1986 to 1992, Björk was in a group called the Sugarcubes, which found fame in the UK and the United States.

Björk launched her solo career in 1993. With a singing style unlike anyone else's, Björk is not afraid to experiment and the results can be soaringly beautiful. Björk also has a strong interest in the visual arts and her stage shows are extraordinary spectacles. She won the Best Actress Award at the 2000 Cannes Film Festival.

In 2010, Björk released an album called *Biophilia*. It featured a new instrument called the Sharpsicord (an automatic accoustic harp), but there was something even more groundbreaking about it. Björk had collaborated with scientists, teachers, app developers, and even an Icelandic choir to create an interactive version. The *Biophilia* app gives users hands-on understanding of music theory and science, is simple to use, and creative.

It is now used in schools in Iceland, Finland, Norway, and Sweden.

Björk cares about the environment and protecting Iceland's landscape. She also supports people around the world who are fighting for their independence.

MIXING DECK

SHARPSICORD

"If you want to make something happen that hasn't happened before, you've got to allow yourself to make a lot of mistakes."

VIRGINIA WOOLF
Writer
(1882–1941)

Adeline Virginia Stephen grew up in a large, unconventional family. Although she didn't have much formal schooling, she read everything and anything in her father's huge library. Virginia's family spent winters in London, UK, and summers in their house on the Cornish coast in southwestern England. Both locations appear in her writing.

In the early 1900s, Virginia became part of a circle of intellectuals, artists, and writers known as the Bloomsbury Group. It included Virginia's older sister Vanessa Bell, who was a painter, and the writer Leonard Woolf, who married Virginia in 1912.

The Woolfs founded Hogarth Press in 1917 and it went on to publish Virginia's novels *Mrs. Dalloway* (1925) and *To the Lighthouse* (1927). Both were groundbreaking, as they experimented with language, and the order in which the story was told. Her work made a huge contribution to literature, and influenced many future writers.

She went on to write *A Room of One's Own* (1929). Here she described the difficulties women face in a society where men hold all the power.

Sadly, Virginia suffered with mental illness her whole life. She felt she could no longer go on, and took her own life in 1941.

"If you do not tell the truth about yourself you cannot tell it about other people."

FRIDA KAHLO
PAINTER
(1907–1954)

Magdalena Carmen Frida Kahlo y Calderón was born in Coyoacán, Mexico. Her father was German and her mother had mixed Spanish and indigenous ancestry. While growing up, Frida spent a lot of time with her father, who was a photographer. She developed a keen eye for detail and took painting classes, but her real ambition was to be a doctor.

In 1925, Frida's life changed when she was involved in an accident—the bus she was on crashed into a streetcar and Frida nearly died. It took her months to recover. While she was stuck in bed, she started to paint, mostly portraits of family, friends, or herself.

In 1927, Frida joined the Mexican Communist Party (PCM). She met the artist Diego Rivera, also in the PCM, the following year. He was 21 years older than Frida and famous for his huge murals, which were inspired by Mayan art. Frida showed him her paintings and he encouraged her to be an artist.

Influenced by Diego, Frida began to celebrate her Mexican heritage. She wore traditional dress and

XOLO (SHORT FOR XOLOITZCUINTLI), A SACRED HAIRLESS DOG

STREETCAR, MEXICO CITY

introduced elements of folk art to her paintings, such as bright textures, bold patterns, and flattened shapes.

In 1929, Frida and Diego married. They spent their first few years of marriage in the United States where Diego was painting. They moved back to Mexico City in 1933.

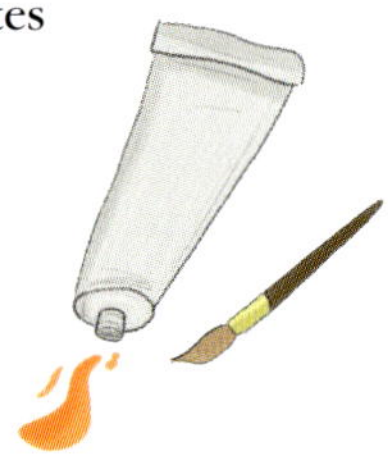

24

> "At the end of the day, we can endure much more than we think we can."

Their home was perfectly suited to their stormy relationship. It was actually two houses—one for each of them—joined by a bridge. The couple had no children but kept a menagerie of pets including monkeys, parrots, and xolos—hairless dogs that had been kept by the ancient Maya and Aztecs.

In 1938, Frida had her first solo exhibition in New York City. She was finding international success as an artist, but her marriage to Diego was crumbling. They divorced in 1939 and Frida moved back to her childhood home, where she created some of her most vulnerable paintings.

In 1940, Frida and Diego remarried and they stayed married until her death. Frida spent her last years in extreme pain because of damage from the 1925 accident. She wore steel corsets and had many operations. In the end, she could not stand or walk, but she still painted.

Frida left behind many great artworks. She expressed her Mexican culture and above all she explored difficult feelings, such as pain, from a female viewpoint.

SIMONE DE BEAUVOIR
Writer and Philosopher
(1908–1986)

In the early 1900s, many French girls grew up hoping to marry well, rather than earn money for themselves. It was traditional for brides to enter marriage with a sum of money called a dowry. Those from prosperous families had larger dowries, so they could be choosier about who they married.

Simone de Beauvoir was born into a middle-class family in Paris. Her father lost most of the family fortune just after World War I. Rather than making Simone hunt for a husband with a pitiful dowry, he decided to spend the little money they had on her education.

The family lived very frugally and their sacrifices paid off. Simone enjoyed studying and had a sharp mind. In 1929, she left the Sorbonne university in Paris with a degree in philosophy.

For the next 14 years Simone supported herself by teaching. She worked in high schools in Marseille, Rouen, and Paris. In 1943, her first novel, *She Came to Stay*, was published and Simone was finally able to become a full-time writer.

Simone is best known not for her novels but for her philosophical work *The Second Sex* (1949), which became a global best seller. She argued that through history societies had treated women as a "second sex," expecting

THE SORBONNE

them to live and behave in a way that suited the interests of men. As wives and mothers, women put the needs of their husbands and children before their own. Simone called for a future where men and women were treated as equals.

Simone lived by the ideas in *The Second Sex*. She met the philosopher Jean-Paul Sartre while she was at university and they had a lifelong relationship. They never married, shared a home, or had children. They read each other's work and went on trips together. They also agreed that each of them was free to have relationships with other people. They gave each other plenty of space and time so they could write and focus on their careers. Jean-Paul died in 1980 and Simone in 1986. They are buried side by side.

Over the years, Simone produced an impressive number of works, including short stories, essays, travel diaries, and an autobiography. Her 1954 novel *The Mandarins* won the Prix Goncourt for its imaginative writing. In 1975, Simone won the Jerusalem Prize, which is awarded to people who write about freedom.

In the 1970s, she became involved in the feminist movement. She took part in demonstrations, wrote articles, and signed open letters that demanded more rights for women. Simone's greatest gift to women was showing that they can live however they choose and need to be responsible only for themselves.

> *"I am too intelligent, too demanding, and too resourceful for anyone to be able to take charge of me entirely."*

27

JOANNE (J. K.) ROWLING
Writer, Film Producer, and Philanthropist
(b.1965)

Joanne Rowling was born near Bristol, in southwest England, UK. She loved reading from a young age and made up stories for her younger sister, including one about a clever giant rabbit.

Not long after Joanne left university her mother died of multiple sclerosis (MS). She went to teach in Portugal, married, and had a baby. In 1993, she left her husband and moved to Edinburgh.

With no job and a daughter to look after, Joanne decided to write. She did this in local cafés because the baby used to fall asleep on the way. Joanne finished writing *Harry Potter and the Sorcerer's Stone* in 1995. Twelve publishers rejected it before Bloomsbury published it in 1997.

Today, Joanne is the world's most successful author. Her *Harry Potter* series has been translated into 65 languages, turned into movies and a musical, and won numerous awards. Joanne was inspired to write a spin-off series, *Fantastic Beasts*. She has also written novels for adults. In 2000, Queen Elizabeth II made her an Official of the Order of the British Empire (OBE) for her services to children's literature. Joanne is also a philanthropist. She uses her vast wealth to help disadvantaged children, support single parents, fund MS research, and much more.

> "It is impossible to live without failing at something, unless you live so cautiously that you might as well not have lived at all—in which case, you fail by default."

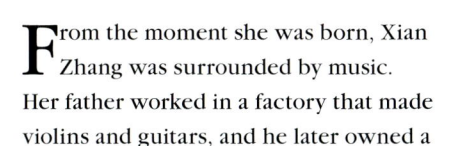

XIAN ZHANG
CONDUCTOR
(b.1973)

From the moment she was born, Xian Zhang was surrounded by music. Her father worked in a factory that made violins and guitars, and he later owned a music shop. Her mother had trained as a pianist.

Xian's mother started to teach her piano when she was three years old. By the time she was six, Xian was playing up to eight hours a day. At 13 she left her home city of Dandong, China, to study music in Beijing. She wanted to be a concert pianist, but her teacher at the conservatory (music school) said her hands were too small. She decided to be a conductor instead.

Xian was just 19 the first time she led an orchestra. Her teacher encouraged her to conduct a rehearsal at the Central Opera House in Beijing. Xian did such an outstanding job that she was asked to come back.

In 1998, Xian went to the United States to study for her PhD in Cincinnati, Ohio. In 2002, she won the first Maazel-

"I was lucky in that what my parents wanted me to do and trained me for was what I wanted to do."

Vilr Conductor's Competition, which was founded to support up-and-coming conductors. She joined the New York Philharmonic Orchestra as an understudy and went on to be associate conductor.

Since then, Xian has been in demand all over the world. She has conducted in Milan, Amsterdam, Dresden, London, Cardiff, and New Jersey. In the very male world of conducting, she is an inspiration.

Arundhati Roy
Writer and Activist
(b.1961)

Suzanna Arundhati Roy was born in Assam, northeastern India. Her Hindu father ran a tea plantation. Her mother Mary was from a Syrian Christian community in Kerala, southern India.

When Arundhati was two years old, her parents separated and her mother moved back to Kerala with the children. Arundhati's grandparents had disapproved of their daughter's mixed marriage to a Hindu and they turned her away. Mary took the children to a cottage her father owned 90 miles (150 km) away. It was a time of hardship. Their mother was ill, so Arundhati and her older brother had to beg for food. They returned to Kerala three years later and Mary became a teacher.

Arundhati went to boarding school at ten, then moved to Delhi when she was 16. She had no money and lived in slums. Arundhati studied architecture because she wanted to know how to design cheap, sustainable housing, but she became downhearted and eventually chose to be a writer instead.

Arundhati had an acting part in *Massey Sahib* (1985), a film about mixed marriage and discrimination directed and written by Pradip Krishen. Arundhati went on to collaborate with Pradip on scripts for a television series and a couple of films.

In 1997, Arundhati's first novel, *The God of Small Things*, was published. Written as a series of flashbacks, it told the story of a twin brother and sister growing up in Kerala. They witness violence and injustice because of the caste system (the Indian way of grouping the people in society by race). Its character Velutha is an "untouchable" from the lowest caste.

In 1997, *The God of Small Things* won the Man Booker, a prize that had never been awarded to an Indian woman before. Arundhati donated her prize money and royalties to human rights charities.

To her readers' surprise, Arundhati did not publish another novel for 20 years.

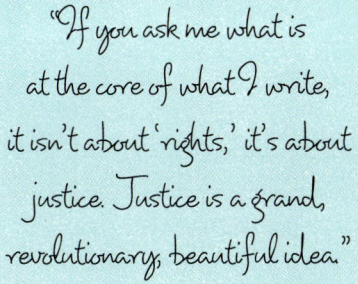

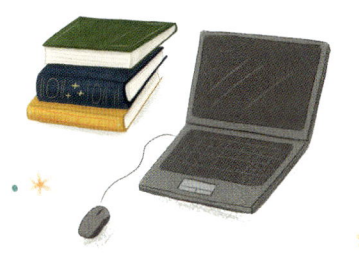

After experiencing hopeless poverty as a girl, Arundhati was sensitive to society's treatment of its most vulnerable citizens. In the booming Indian economy, new money was often made by exploiting the poor or damaging the environment—and it almost all ended up in rich people's pockets.

Arundhati's political writings exposed the dangers of greed and globalization and supported issues such as Kashmiri independence. In 2004, she was awarded the Sydney Peace Prize and in 2014 she was on the *Time* list of the 100 Most Influential People in the World. Arundhati's long-awaited second novel, *The Ministry of Utmost Happiness*, appeared in 2017.

"If you ask me what is at the core of what I write, it isn't about 'rights,' it's about justice. Justice is a grand, revolutionary, beautiful idea."

MAYA ANGELOU

Writer, Singer, Actor, and Activist

(1928–2014)

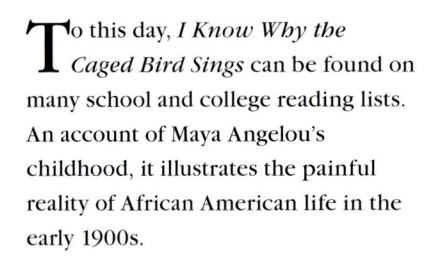

To this day, *I Know Why the Caged Bird Sings* can be found on many school and college reading lists. An account of Maya Angelou's childhood, it illustrates the painful reality of African American life in the early 1900s.

Born Marguerite Annie Johnson in St. Louis, Missouri, Maya was sent to rural Arkansas with her brother when she was three years old. Her parents had divorced, and her father wanted the children to live with his mother.

Arkansas was segregated at that time, which meant that black citizens could not share the same public spaces as white people and were regularly discriminated against. Schools put black children at a disadvantage.

Maya's autobiography described a distressing incident that happened when she was eight years old. She was abused by a family friend. Maya was brave enough to tell someone and her attacker was caught, tried, and imprisoned. Unfortunately, he was released a day later and murdered. Maya felt so guilty about his death that she didn't speak for five years. She finally found her voice again thanks to help from a kind woman called Mrs. Flowers.

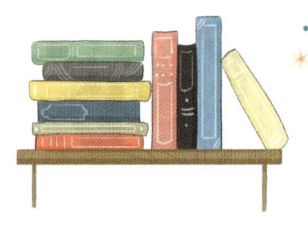

Maya moved to San Francisco with her mother and brother when she was 14. While she was still finishing school she worked on the streetcars. She was the city's first black female conductor. Maya had a baby son when she was 17, just after leaving school.

When she was 20 years old, Maya started training as a dancer and decided to use her nickname "Maya" as her professional name. She toured Europe in musicals and found roles in plays in New York City.

From 1961 to 1965, Maya spent time in

"It's one of the greatest gifts you can give yourself, to forgive. Forgive everybody."

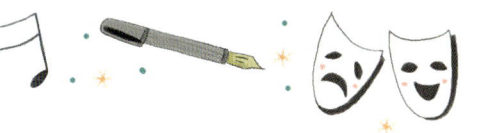

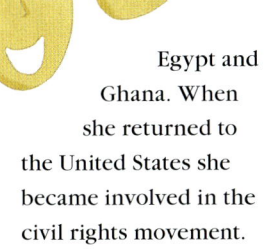

Egypt and Ghana. When she returned to the United States she became involved in the civil rights movement.

Maya worked closely with the civil rights leaders Martin Luther King Jr. and Malcom X. When Martin Luther King Jr. was assassinated in 1968, Maya was devastated. She put her energy into writing.

I Know Why the Caged Bird Sings, published in 1969, was one of seven autobiographies that Maya wrote during her lifetime. Some of Maya's fans believe that these are her most important works because they look at black identity.

Maya's first collection of poems appeared in 1971 and was nominated for a Pulitzer Prize. The following year Maya became the first African-American woman to have written the screenplay for a feature film. In 2011, President Barack Obama presented Maya with the Presidential Medal of Freedom.

LAVERNE COX
ACTOR AND ACTIVIST
(b.1972)

Laverne Cox is a successful actor, producer, writer, and activist. She is transgender, meaning that her identity and gender is not the same as her birth sex. She was *Time* magazine's first openly transgender cover star and one of the first in the transgender community to find worldwide fame.

Laverne was born in Alabama, and raised by her mother and grandmother. She was bullied at school for appearing feminine. Laverne found acting fame in 2013, when Netflix broadcast the first season of *Orange Is the New Black*. She played the transgender inmate and prison hairdresser Sophia. Laverne travels widely to raise awareness and talk about how racism and poverty make life even more difficult for people in LGBTQ+ communities.

"My life changed when I realized I deserve to be seen, to dream, to be fully included, always striving to bring my full humanity."

MARIA CALLAS
Opera Singer
(1923–1977)

"There are two people in me, [...] I would like to be Maria, but there is the Callas that I have to live up to."

Maria Callas was born in New York City to Greek parents. When she was 13, she moved to Athens, Greece, with her mother and older sister. The great Spanish soprano Elvira de Hidalgo taught her to sing and after World War II suggested that she move to Italy. Maria built up her career there. By the 1950s, she was performing in the world's leading opera houses, including La Scala in Milan, the Royal Opera House in London, and the Metropolitan Opera in New York City. Maria stopped singing live in 1965.

Maria's voice divided opinion. Some said that she sang like an angel, while others criticized her technique and "wobbly" high notes. She could also be difficult to work with. But everyone agreed that she brought opera to life like no other.

MILLO CASTRO ZALDARRIAGA
DRUMMER
(b.1922)

Growing up in Cuba in the 1920s and 1930s, Millo Castro Zaldarriaga, a young girl of Cuban, Chinese, and African heritage, dreamed of being a bongo player. The drums were an important part of Cuban culture, just as they are today. But at that time only boys and men were allowed to play them. Millo's father refused to pay for her to have lessons but she was so persistent that he eventually gave in.

Millo formed an all-girl band when she was 10, played at American President Franklin D. Roosevelt's birthday party at 15, and later toured the world as a jazz musician. Millo had rhythm, talent, and determination—but above all, she had the courage to follow her dreams.

"I meet many young people who have been discouraged from pursuing a career in the creative field. It takes courage to overcome that resistance."

- Rafael Lopez, illustrator of *Dream Drum Girl* about Millo Castro Zaldarriaga.

GRACE COSSINGTON SMITH
Painter
(1892–1984)

Born Grace Smith in Sydney, Australia, Grace studied art in England and Germany as well as her home city. She became an artist when most painters were men. Grace's style of painting was post-impressionist—it emphasized the basic shapes of figures and scenery and used striking shades and thick brushstrokes to capture the effects of the light. Her 1915 work *The Sock Knitter* is Australia's first post-impressionist painting.

Grace painted many pictures of Sydney, including the building of its iconic bridge. Her work was admired by other painters, but ignored by the critics. In 1973, Grace was given an Order of the British Empire (OBE). She admitted that she was glad she hadn't received much attention during her career because it had allowed her to focus on how she wanted to paint.

"My chief interest I think has always been color, but not flat crude color, it must be color within color, it has to shine, light must be in it"

COCO CHANEL
FASHION DESIGNER AND BUSINESSWOMAN
(1883–1971)

The "little black dress," the neat tweed suit, the quilted purse, and the costume pearl necklace … all of these timeless "classics" have one thing in common. They were designed by the groundbreaking fashion designer Coco Chanel.

Born Gabrielle Bonheur Chanel in Saumur, western France, Coco spent her childhood in poverty. When she was 12, her mother died of tuberculosis. Coco and her two sisters were sent to a convent, while their brothers became farmhands.

Coco learned to sew at the convent. When she left at age 18, she went to work as a seamstress and bar singer in the city of Moulins. It was around this time that she took the name "Coco."

Coco made some rich friends in Moulins, including the French socialite Étienne Balsan and English polo player Boy Capel. These men helped her to fund her first businesses: a hat shop that she opened in Paris in 1910 and a clothing boutique in the fashionable

> "The most courageous act is still to think for yourself. Aloud."

38

seaside resort of Deauville in 1913.

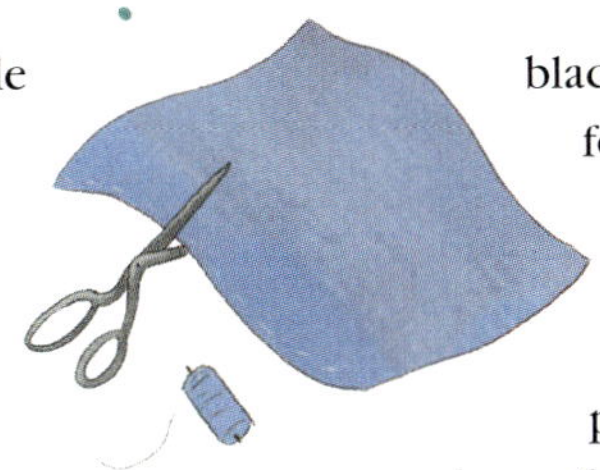

At the time women were expected to wear long, frilled dresses in heavy fabrics, over tight, restrictive corsets. Coco wanted to make simple, elegant clothing in comfortable fabrics and she drew her inspiration from menswear. Her sailor's clothes and shorter skirts gave women more freedom and captured the spirit of the time.

Coco's boutique was a runaway success and she soon opened stores in Biarritz and Paris. By 1919 she was a registered couturier (fashion designer).

One of Coco's biggest successes was Chanel No. 5, the perfume that she launched in 1922. No fashion house had released its own branded scent before. Chanel No. 5 was also the first mass-produced perfume with multiple "notes" rather than a single scent. It is still a best seller today.

In 1926, Coco created the little black dress—a simple dress suitable for any occasion. Coco was responsible for making black—associated with mourning—chic and fashionable. It was perfect for showing off strings of large, fake pearls and other accessories.

By the late 1930s, the House of Chanel had 4,000 employees. Coco closed her business at the start of World War II and did not reopen until 1954. She updated her tweed suit, launched the "hands-free" Chanel bag with its long strap of gold chain, and rescued women from high heels with her flat, two-tone ballet pumps.

Coco died in 1971, but her bold ideas lived on. She revolutionized fashion and the Western woman's wardrobe, giving them clothes that suited their new, active lifestyles.

ZAHA HADID
Architect
(1950–2016)

When Zaha Hadid died suddenly in March 2016, it wasn't just fellow architects who mourned. Zaha's inspirational, monumental, and unique buildings had shaped cities and landscapes all over the world. Her creations were part of people's lives. Unusually for an architect, Zaha had made the leap from unconventional outsider to famous and "mainstream" in a very short space of time.

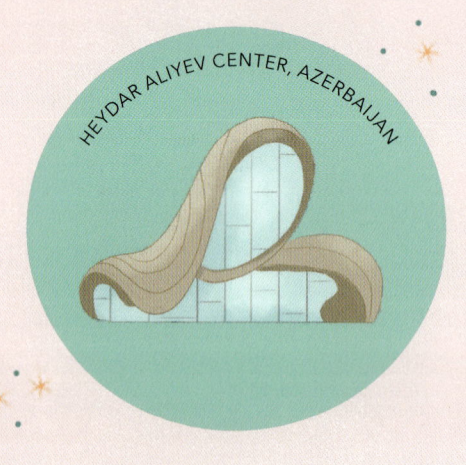

HEYDAR ALIYEV CENTER, AZERBAIJAN

Zaha was born in Baghdad, Iraq. Her family were Sunni Muslims and she was one of three children. Her father was a prominent politician who believed in democracy and social reform. Her mother was an artist. Zaha went to schools in Baghdad, England, and Switzerland. She gained a degree in mathematics from the American University of Beirut, Lebanon.

As Zaha was growing up, she became interested in architecture. It was a time of great optimism, when forward-thinking architects were rebuilding cities after the devastation of World War II.

In 1972, Zaha moved to London, UK, to study at the Architectural Association (AA). Her tutors included the architects Rem Koolhaas and Elia Zenghelis, who were known for their daring and intelligent work. The AA had a reputation for radical architecture that looked amazing on paper but was not actually buildable. Zaha excelled there but, unlike many fellow students, she wanted to construct her creations.

Zaha opened her own architectural firm in London in 1980. One of her first projects was a small fire station on the German–Swiss border. Its dramatic, sloping concrete walls at irregular angles and large, frameless windows catapulted her to fame. Today the building is used for art exhibitions.

Over Zaha's career, technology improved and materials could be used in new ways. Zaha refined her trademark style, creating curvy buildings such as the London Aquatics Centre for the 2012 Olympic Games and the Heydar Aliyev Center, an arts complex in Azerbaijan. In 2004, Zaha became the first woman

LONDON AQUATIC CENTRE

to win the prestigious Pritzker Architecture Prize, which recognizes architects who show great vision and talent. In 2010, she was awarded the Royal Institute of British Architects (RIBA) Stirling Prize for the MAXXI, a museum of modern art and architecture in Rome, Italy. She was made Dame Commander of the Order of the British Empire (OBE) in 2012.

Zaha proudly collected the RIBA Royal Gold Medal just eight weeks before her sudden heart attack. She was the first woman to receive the prize, which acknowledges a lifetime of great architecture.

"Yes, I am a feminist, because I see all women as smart, gifted, and tough."

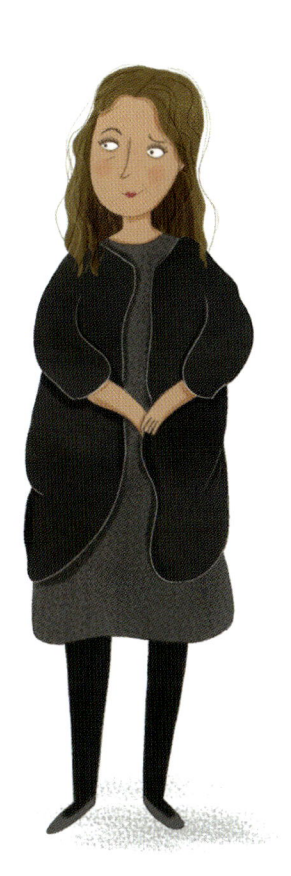

QUIZ

1. What was the first novel that Jane Austen wrote and published?

2. How old was Nina Simone when she first started playing the organ?

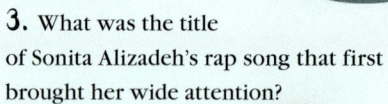

3. What was the title of Sonita Alizadeh's rap song that first brought her wide attention?

4. Where was Joan Armatrading born?

5. Where was the hideout that Anne Frank's father built to protect them?

6. What special occasion did Kiri Te Kanawa sing at in 1981?

7. In which year did Angelina Jolie win her first Golden Globe?

8. What award was Nadežda Petrović given for her work with the Red Cross?

9. What instrument was Melba Liston famous for playing?

10. What was the name of the all-female group that was formed by Miriam Makeba?

11. How old was Björk when she recorded her first solo album?

12. What was the name of the publishing house founded by Virginia and Leonard Woolf?

13. What was Frida Kahlo's first ambition?

14. What was the title of Simone de Beauvoir's famous work?

15. Which publisher published J. K. Rowling's *Harry Potter*, when 12 others had refused it?

16. Why was Xian Zang told she would not be a concert pianist?

1. Sense and Sensibility, 2. 3; 3. Brides for Sale; 4. St. Kitts; 5. Behind a bookcase; 6. The Wedding of Prince Charles and Lady Diana Spencer; 7. 1998; 8. Medal for Bravery; 9. trombone; 10. The Skylarks; 11. 11; 12. Hogarth Press; 13. To be a doctor; 14. The Second Sex; 15. Bloomsbury; 16. Because her hands were too small!

RESEARCH PROJECT

Now that you have read about all of these inspiring women, it's time to take a look closer to home. The women in your life have incredible stories to tell, too!

Speak to your mom, aunt, grandmother, caregiver, or teacher to discover their stories and their own experiences. Here are some questions to get you started:

- WHO WERE YOUR FEMALE HEROES GROWING UP?
- WHAT ACHIEVEMENT ARE YOU MOST PROUD OF?
- WHO HAS SUPPORTED YOU THROUGH YOUR LIFE?
- HAVE YOU OVERCOME DIFFICULTIES TO ACHIEVE YOUR GOALS?
- WHICH WOMEN DO YOU ADMIRE TODAY?
- WHAT ARE THE MOST IMPORTANT LESSONS THAT YOU HAVE LEARNED?
- WHAT IS THE BEST JOB YOU HAVE HAD?
- WHAT ADVICE WOULD YOU GIVE YOUNG WOMEN TODAY?
- AS A CHILD, WHAT DID YOU WANT TO BE WHEN YOU GREW UP?
- WHAT WAS YOUR EXPERIENCE IN SCHOOL?
- WHERE DID YOU GROW UP?

Listen carefully to the answers that people give. It is important to record information correctly when people are speaking. If you are going to record what someone tells you, make sure that you ask permission first.

When you have finished asking questions, you can write a report about the person you talked to. You could even include a portrait of them!

Remember that some people might not want to answer one or more of your questions. If that's the case, be respectful and move on to the next question, or simply ask someone else who is willing to share their story. If you want to record their answers, you must ask for permission first.

GLOSSARY

CIVIL RIGHTS MOVEMENT
The group of people who came together in the 1950s and 1960s to end racial inequality. It began in the United States.

DEMOCRACY
A system of government whereby the people have a say, usually by electing representatives.

DISCRIMINATION
Treating people differently because of a certain difference between them, for example, their gender, race, religion, or political beliefs.

ABOLISH
To put an end to a system.

ARCHITECTURE
The art and science of designing and constructing buildings.

ASSASSINATE
To murder an important person for political or religious reasons.

AUSCHWITZ
The name of a Nazi concentration camp during World War II.

AUTOBIOGRAPHY
A book someone writes about their own life.

BAPTIST
A member of a branch of the Christian faith.

POVERTY
Living in a state of extreme poorness.

REFUGEE
Someone who has been forced to flee their home country because of war or persecution.

SEGREGATION
Separating people into groups, usually according to their race.

SOPRANO
The highest singing voice.

TOWNSHIP
A South African term for an area outside of a city that has a high black population.

EMIGRATE
To leave your home country and live in another.

FRUGAL
To live without spending much money.

INDIGINOUS
Originating in, or native to, a particular area.

MAORI
The name for the aboriginal people of New Zealand.

PERSECUTION
When a person is treated unfairly or with hostility because of their race, religion, or political beliefs.

FURTHER INFORMATION

BOOKS

ANTHOLOGY OF AMAZING WOMEN
by Sandra Lawrence and Nathan Collins (20 Watt, 2018)

DRUM DREAM GIRL: HOW ONE GIRL'S COURAGE CHANGED MUSIC
by Margarita Engle (Houghton Mifflin, 2015)

F IS FOR FEMINISM
by Carolyn Suzuki (Ladybird, 2019)

FANTASTICALLY GREAT WOMEN WHO CHANGED THE WORLD
by Kate Pankhurst (Bloomsbury Children's Books, 2016)

GIRLS CAN DO ANYTHING! by Caryl Hart (Scholastic, 2018)

GIRLS WHO CHANGED THE WORLD
by Michelle Roehm McCann (Simon & Schuster, 2018)

HER STORY: 50 WOMEN AND GIRLS WHO SHOOK THE WORLD
by Katherine Halligan (Nosy Crow, 2018)

I KNOW A WOMAN: THE INSPIRING CONNECTIONS BETWEEN THE WOMEN WHO HAVE CHANGED OUR WORLD
by Kate Hodges (Aurum Press, 2018)

THE DIARY OF A YOUNG GIRL
by Anne Frank (Puffin, 2007)

THE WORLD IS NOT A RECTANGLE: A PORTRAIT OF ARCHITECT ZAHA HADID
by Jeanette Winter (Beach Lane Books, 2017)

WOMEN IN ART: LITTLE PEOPLE, BIG DREAMS
by Isabel Sanchez Vegara (Lincoln Children's Books, 2018)

YOUNG GIFTED AND BLACK: MEET 52 BLACK HEROES FROM PAST AND PRESENT
by Jamia Wilson (Wide Eyed Editions, 2019)

WEBSITES

The Amazing Women in History website aims to bring together all the amazing women left out of history books.
amazingwomeninhistory.com/

The Inspirational Women Series website displays a series on interviews with women leaders from around the world.
inspirationalwomenseries.org/

Have a look at the section on Women Who Made History on the English Heritage website.
english-heritage.org.uk/learn/histories/women-in-history/

Find out who has won the prestigious Nobel Prize. They are awarded for Physics, Chemistry, Medicine, Literature, and contributing to world peace.
nobelprize.org/

Find out more about the Kiri Te Kanawa Foundation here:
kiritekanawa.org/

Use these webpages to learn more about UNESCO Goodwill Ambassadors. The United Nations Educational, Scientific, and Cultural Organization appoint key people to spread the ideals of the organization. Goodwill Ambassadors help to raise the profile of the organizations' initiatives.
unesco.org/new/en/goodwill-ambassadors/goodwill-ambassadors/

Explore Bjork's Biophilia Education Project here:
biophiliaeducational.org/

Have a look at the website of the Man Booker Prize to find out how many women have won.
themanbookerprize.com/

Each year, *Time* magazine releases a list of their 100 Most Influential People. Take a look here:
time.com/collection/most-influential-people-2018/

Publisher's note to educators and parents: Our editors have carefully reviewed these websites to ensure that they are suitable for students. Many websites change frequently, however, and we cannot guarantee that a site's future contents will continue to meet our high standards of quality and educational value. Be advised that students should be closely supervised whenever they access the internet.

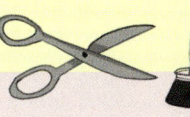

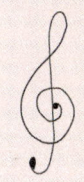

47

INDEX

A Room of One's Own 23
activist 7, 10, 12, 17, 20, 30, 32, 34
actor 17, 22, 32, 34
Afghanistan 12
Alabama, 34
Alizadeh, Sonita 12, 42
Amsterdam, Netherlands 14
Angelou, Maya 32-33
apartheid 20
architecture 30, 40
Armatrading, Joan 13, 42
Assam, India 30
Austen, Jane 8, 42

Baghdad, Iraq 40
Belafonte, Harry 21
Birmingham, UK 13
Björk 2, 22, 42
Bloomsbury Group 23
Brides for Sale (song) 12
Bristol, UK 28

Čačak, Serbia 18
Callas, Maria 35
Chanel, Coco 38-39
civil rights movement 11, 21, 33
conductor 29
Cossington Smith, Grace 4, 37
Cox, Laverne 3, 34
Coyoacán, Mexico 24
Cuba 36

dance 6
Dandong, China 29
de Beauvoir, Simone 26, 42
drama 6

Elliot, George 7
Emma 8

Fantastic Beasts series 28
film 6, 8, 9, 12, 20, 22, 28, 30, 33
Frank, Anne 2, 14-15, 42
Frankfurt, Germany 14

Gaye, Marvin 19
Ghaemmaghami, Rokhsareh 12
Gillespie, Dizzy 19

Hadid, Zaha 7, 40-41
Harry Potter series 28, 42

I Know Why the Caged Bird Sings 32, 33
Iran 12

Johannesburg, South Africa 20
Jolie, Angelina 6, 17, 42

Kanawa, Kiri Te 16, 42
Kahlo, Frida 5, 24-25, 42
King, Jr., Martin Luther 33

Liston, Melba 4, 19, 42
London, UK 16, 23
Los Angeles, 17

Makeba, Miriam 20-21, 42
Mandela, Nelson 21
Mississippi, 9
Missouri, 19, 32
Mrs. Dalloway 23
Munich, Germany 18
music 6, 8, 19, 22

New York City, 9, 20, 25, 32, 35
New Zealand 16
North Carolina, 10

Obama, Barack 33
opera 9, 16, 35

painting 6, 8, 18, 24, 37
Paris, France 26
Petrović, Nadežda 18, 42
philosopher 26
photography 6
Price, Leontyne 9
Pride and Prejudice 8

refugees 12
Reykjavik, Iceland 22
Rivera, Diego 24
Roosevelt, Franklin D 36
Rowling, Joanne, K. 28, 42
Roy, Arundhati 30-31

St. Kitts 13
Sartre, Jean-Paul 27

segregation 9, 11, 20
Sense and Sensibility 8
Sharpeville massacre 21
Simone, Nina 10-11, 42
singer 16, 20, 22, 32, 35, 38
songwriter 13
Supremes, The 19
Sydney, Australia 37

teaching 18, 22, 26, 30
The God of Small Things 30
The Ministry of Utmost Happiness 31
The Second Sex 27
To the Lighthouse 23

Utah, 12

Woolf, Virginia 7, 23, 42
World War I 18, 26
World War II 14, 35, 40
writer 14, 23, 26, 28, 30, 32, 34

Zaldarriaga, Millo Castro 36
Zhang, Xian 29, 42

48